SHERBE-SHERBERT

SHERBE-SHERBERT Adult Coloring Book Vol. 1

ISBN: 979-8-9902578-1-8

Copyright 2024 Angelic Reign Inc. All rights reserved universally and beyond.

No part of this book may be reproduced or copied in any manner without prior written permission from the publisher. For more information contact us at angelicreigninc2004@outlook.com

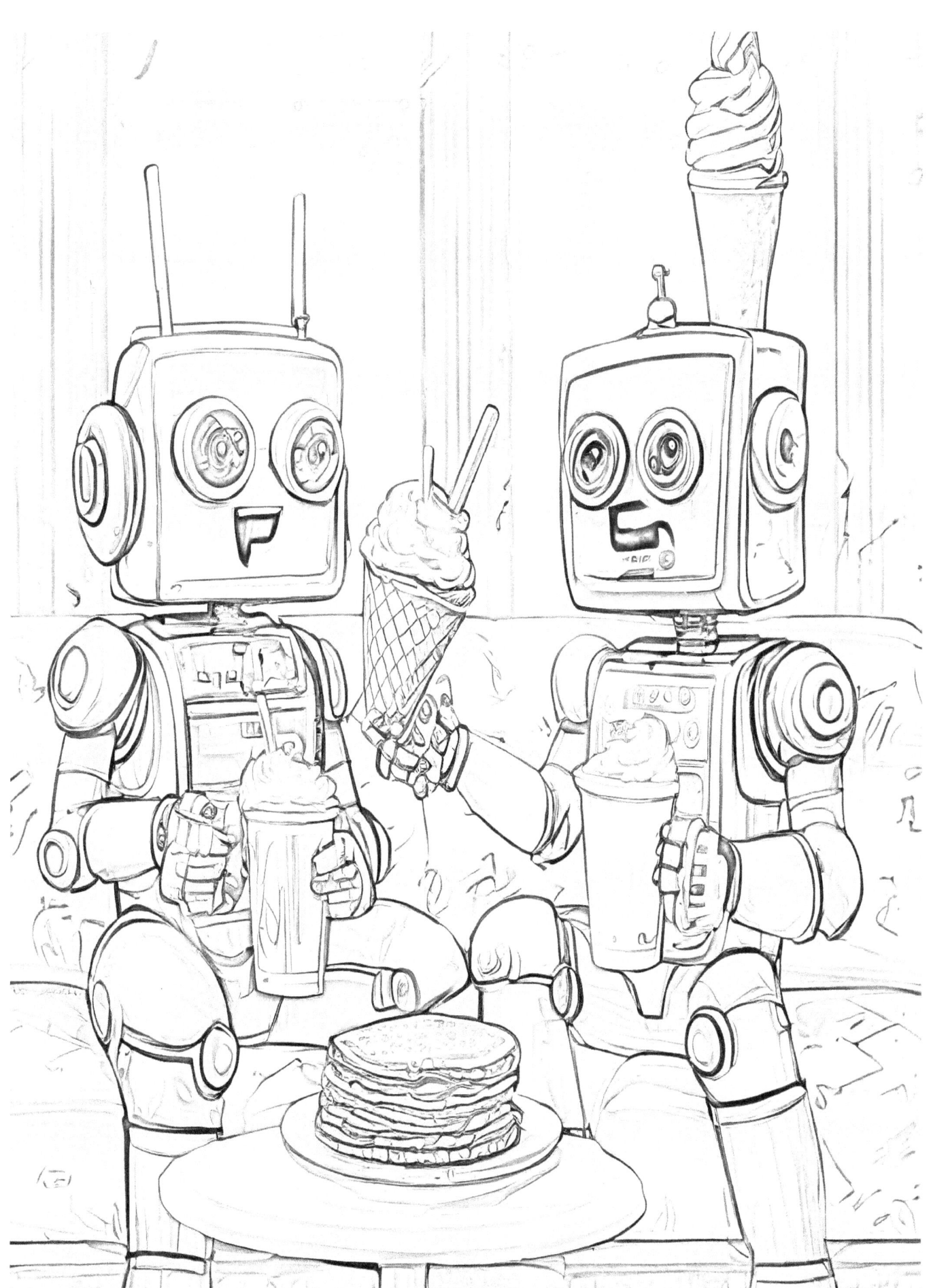

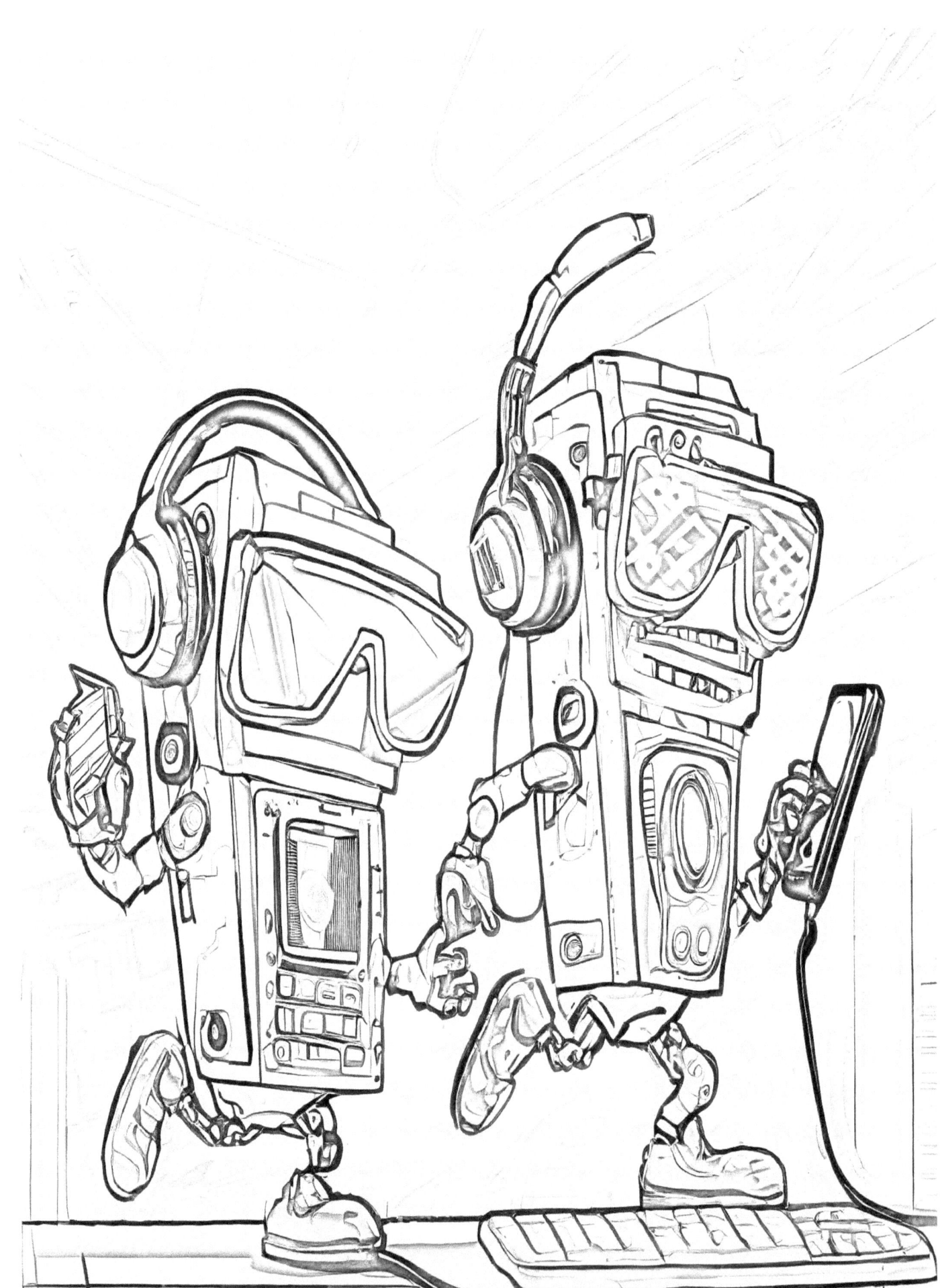

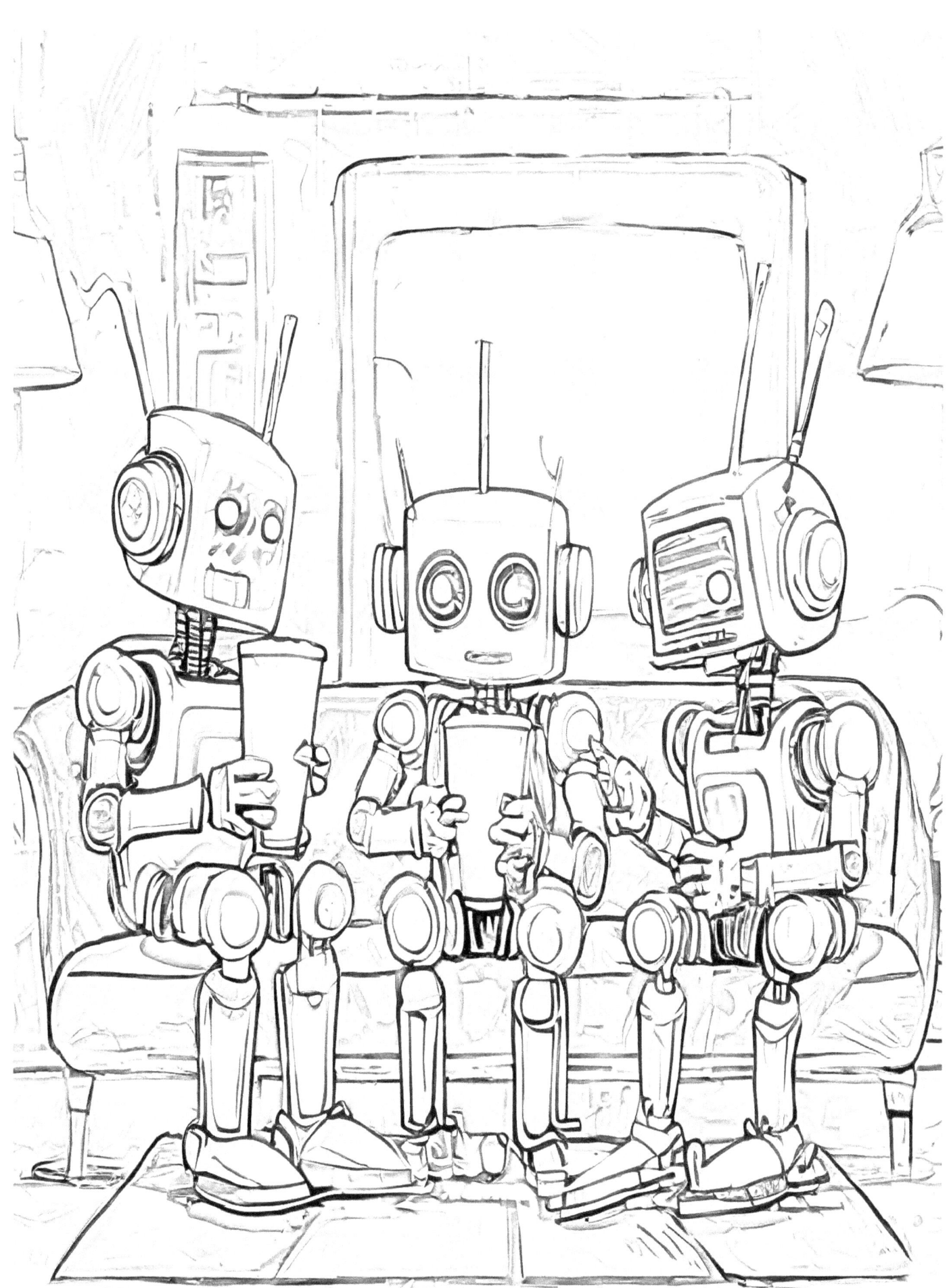

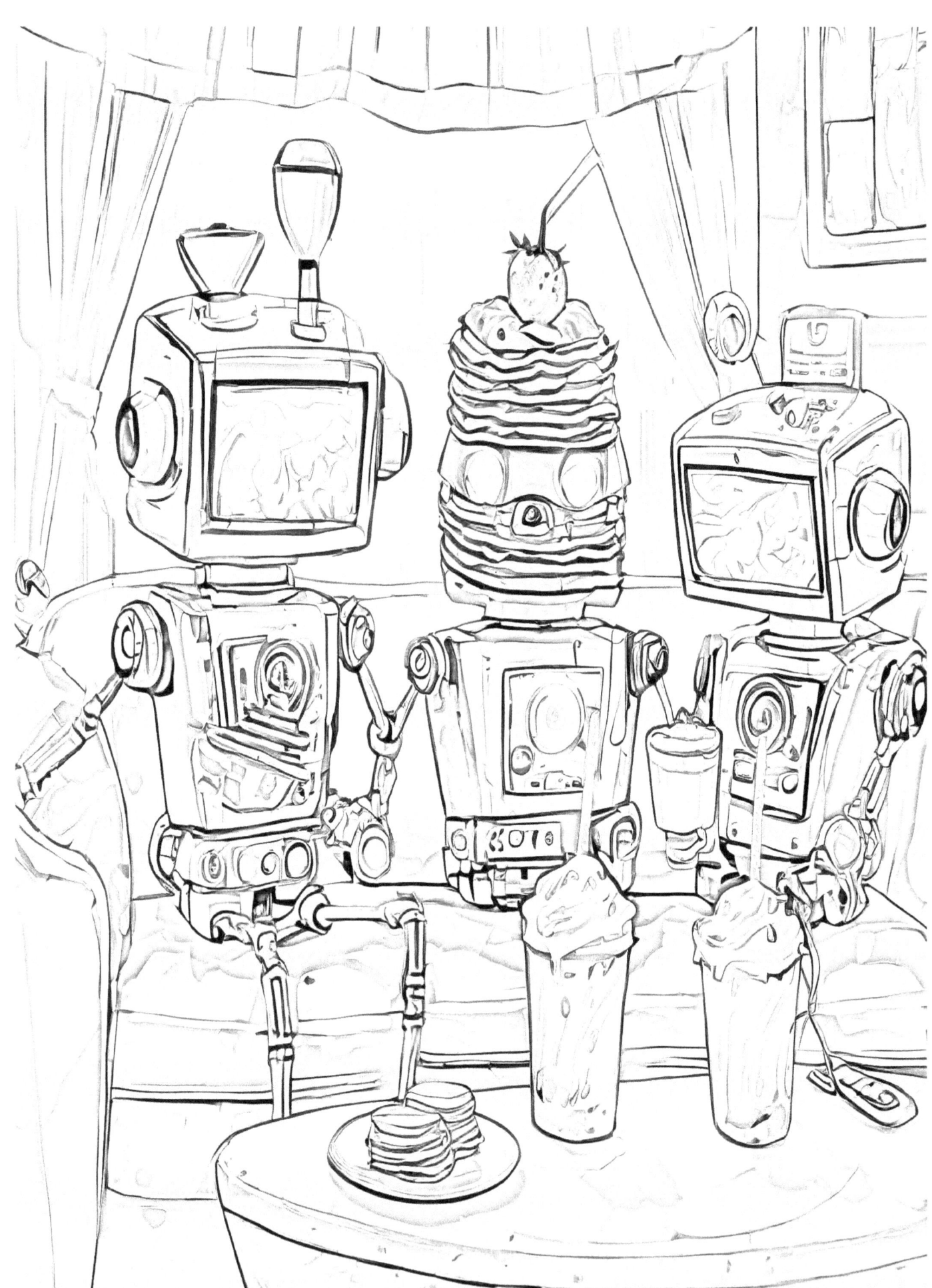

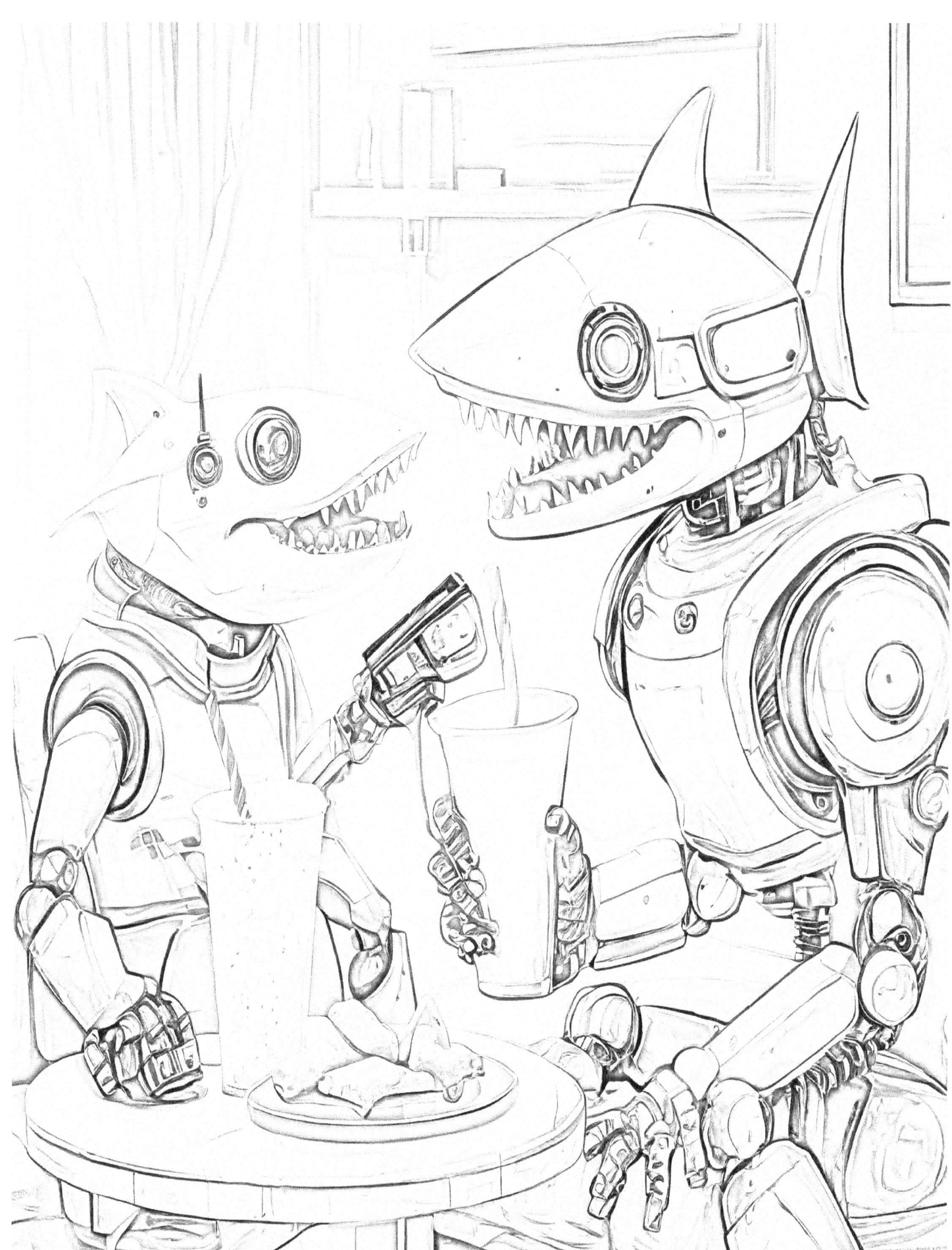

SHERBE-SHERBERT

If you enjoyed Sherbe-Sherbert. Vol.1. You may also like Vol.2; Vol.3; and more.

Copyright 2024 Angelic Reign Inc. All rights reserved universally and beyond. No part of this book may be reproduced or copied in any manner without prior written permission from the publisher. For more information contact us at angelicreigninc2004@outlook.com

www.ingramcontent.com/pod-product-compliance
Lightning Source LLC
Chambersburg PA
CBHW041426040426
42444CB00022B/3481